Stage Fright

**Other Apple® paperbacks
you will enjoy:**

Stage Fright

Ann M. Martin

Drawings by Blanche Sims

AN
APPLE®
PAPERBACK

SCHOLASTIC INC.
New York Toronto London Auckland Sydney

ISBN 0-590-33758-0

12 11 10 9 8 7 6 5 4 3 2 1   4   6 7 8 9/8 0 1/9

Printed in the U.S.A.   28

Mom,
this book is for you
because I love you.

Contents

Stage Fright

1.

The Birthday Party

"Me, me, me!"

"Ooh, ooh, ooh!"

"Pick me, pick me!"

I looked around. Every single girl at Carol's tenth birthday party was waving her hand wildly. They all wanted to be picked as the magician's assistant.

Except me.

I was hoping nobody would even see me. I didn't want to be the magician's assistant. I'd rather have eaten Brussels sprouts for the rest of my life. No kidding.

We were sitting on folding chairs in my cousin Carol's backyard. I was in the last row next to Wendy, my very best friend in the whole world.

Wendy lives next door to me, and Carol lives

across the street. Carol turned ten first, Wendy'd catch up in two months, and I'd catch up in four months.

Anyway, Wendy and I were in the back row. I always choose the back row if I can. When you're up front, people can see you, and I hate being seen.

The magician's name was Dr. Sorcery. Dr. Sorcery was standing in front of us. He was wearing a black top hat with a yellow flower stuck in the band, and a black coat with glittery stars and moons on it.

He looked around at all the hands. "Let's see," he said.

"Me! Me, me!" That was Wendy. She was waving harder than anybody. She just loves being seen.

I slumped down in my chair so far I almost slid onto the ground.

Finally the magician made a choice. "Okay," he said. "You in the blue dress."

That was Wendy.

I sighed with relief.

Wendy ran around the chairs to Dr. Sorcery. When she reached him, he shook her hand and said, "Hello, young lady. What's your name?"

"Wendy," she replied, grinning.

I would have died.

But Wendy enjoyed it.

"Well," said Dr. Sorcery, "starting right now,

you're not Wendy, you're Magicadabra, my faithful assistant."

Everybody giggled. Wendy grinned even harder. Sometimes I wish I could be just like Wendy. Sometimes.

Dr. Sorcery gave Wendy a bright blue cape to wear and a silvery crown-thing for her hair. Then she helped him by holding up rings and scarves and tubes. She pulled a bouquet of flowers out of an empty black velvet bag. She fanned out a deck of cards so he could do mind reading. And she broke an egg into his hat.

At last the show was over. Everybody clapped while Dr. Sorcery and Magicadabra took their bows. Wendy gave back the cape and crown. Then my aunt Martha, Carol's mother, said, "Thank you, Dr. Sorcery. Now if everybody will come to the picnic tables, we'll have cake and ice cream."

"Yay!" shouted the girls.

I was glad it was time for cake and ice cream, but I didn't feel like shouting.

I caught up with Wendy as fast as I could. I just had to sit next to her or Carol at the table.

We found seats together at Carol's table. There was a yellow plastic basket full of candies at everybody's place. There was also a little box that turned out to be holding a beaded bracelet and one of those snappers that pops when you pull the ends apart.

As soon as we were sitting down, all the girls began snapping their favors.

Pop! Pop! Bang! It sounded like we were in the middle of a war.

Wendy pulled hers apart with a satisfying *crack!* and examined the prizes inside—a paper party hat, a red ring for her finger, and a fortune on a folded slip of paper. The fortune said: *Spend your money wisely now, and you will be rich later.*

"Wow," said Wendy. "Rich."

She looked longingly at my party favor.

"Want to pop it?" I asked gratefully.

"Really?" asked Wendy. "I can pop it? I'll give you all the stuff inside, okay?"

"Okay," I said.

Wendy snapped mine open and gave me the hat, the ring, and the fortune. My fortune said: *You won't be lonely for long. A handsome stranger will sweep you off your feet by the end of the month.*

Wendy and I giggled. "A handsome stranger," she teased. "Wooo-weee, your first boyfriend!"

"Oh, Wendy," I said. I was probably blushing, but I was laughing, too.

It was right then that Carol suggested, "Hey, let's go around the table, and everybody read your fortune out loud so we can all hear, okay?"

I froze. My tongue glued itself to the roof of my mouth, and my stomach dropped about a foot.

I must have looked awful, because Wendy said, "Sara? What's wrong?"

I glanced at her but didn't say anything.

"Don't you want to read your fortune?" Wendy guessed. She knows me pretty well.

I certainly did not. It's bad enough having to read aloud, but all that stuff about a handsome stranger— the girls would tease me from here to next year.

I managed to shake my head.

"Okay," Wendy said. "I'll take care of it."

I didn't bother to ask how. Just as long as someone was going to take care of it.

Carol read her fortune out loud and everybody laughed. Then Annie, sitting next to Carol, read her fortune, and everybody laughed at her. Two people to go and it would be my turn. What was Wendy going to do?

Ha ha. Hee hee. Everyone was laughing again.

Now it was my turn.

"Okay, Sara," called Carol. "What does yours say?"

Before I could even look at Wendy, she jumped in and said, "You'll never guess what happened. I ate Sara's fortune. It was an accident. It was stuck to this piece of candy—"

"Wendy!" exclaimed Aunt Martha suddenly. She was walking around the table putting a scoop of ice cream on everybody's plate. She stopped with the scooper in midair. "You ate the paper? That could be dangerous. Maybe—"

"Oh, it's all right," Wendy interrupted quickly. "I didn't swallow it or anything. I just sort of chewed it up. I spit most of it out."

"Well, if you're sure . . ."

"I am. Listen, my fortune was great." She read it out loud.

Everybody had forgotten about me and my fortune, and Wendy had saved me from another mess.

What would I do without her?

When we were through reading the fortunes, Aunt Martha and Uncle John brought Carol's cake to the table. We sang three different verses of "Happy Birthday." First we sang the regular "Happy Birthday to you" verse. Then we sang the "How old are you?" verse. The last verse we sang went like this:

> Happy birthday to you.
> You live in a zoo.
> You look like a
>   monkey,
> And smell like one, too!

Aunt Martha and Uncle John looked disgusted at

that part, but Carol just laughed and cut the cake. After we'd stuffed ourselves, it was time to go home.

Aunt Martha handed out goody bags, which we filled with our candy and fortunes and prizes. Wendy and I called goodbye to Carol and wished her one more Happy Birthday. Then we started across the street to my house.

I had survived another party.

But I still had to face my mother.

2.

Fighting

Wendy and I ran through the front door of my house. I was so *glad* to be home, even if I had just been across the street. Home was safe—at least safer than a party.

In the living room, Star and Lucy were curled up on the big couch. They were sleeping as close together as they possibly could. In fact, Star was draped across Lucy's back with his tail in her face. Lucy didn't seem to mind at all.

Next to my parents and Wendy, Star and Lucy are my favorite people, even though they are cats. We got Lucy first. She has long, fluffy fur and came from a pet shop. She's lazy and loveable and purrs practically nonstop. Star came later. We opened the front door one winter morning and he was just sitting on our porch. It was as if the house and Mom and Daddy and I belonged to him already. So we invited him in and he stayed. Star is not very handsome— he's lumpy and sort of fat, and he has spots in all the wrong places, but he makes up for his looks by being the world's biggest show-off.

I dashed across the living room and plopped down on the couch with a bounce. Lucy didn't budge. Star opened one eye, looked at me, and closed the eye again.

"Hi, Kiddos," I said. I have about half a million nicknames for the cats. Star is called Starbo, Starfur, Staz, Stazzy, Starro, and sometimes Mouse. I don't know why. Lucy is called Lucille, Luce, Lulu, Looie, Looz, and Purr-woman. Together they are called Kiddos, Babies, Cat People, the Cat Kids, and the King and Queen of Fur.

I bent over and buried my face against Lucy. "How are you guys? Did you miss me?"

Wendy rolled her eyes. She likes Lucy and Star okay, but not the way I do. Maybe it's because she doesn't have any pets at home. She has a brother and sister instead.

Wendy sat down next to me and patted Lucy. Luce's fur really is fantastic. I wonder if old Starbo ever gets jealous of it.

Wendy and I were sitting, still patting the cats,

when Mom and Daddy came in.

"Well," said Mom brightly. "Hi, Wendy. How was the party, you two?"

I paused.

Here's the thing about parties: I don't like them.

Here's the thing about my mother: she wants me to love them.

Here's the thing about Wendy: she *loves* parties, and my mother thinks that's just wonderful.

Finally I said carefully, "It was okay."

"Oh, Sara," said my mother. "Can't you be a little more enthusiastic?"

I sighed. If I got all enthusiastic, I'd be lying.

When I didn't say anything, my mother let out a pretty big sigh of her own.

She'd never understand that I simply didn't like parties. I knew she only wanted me to like them because she thought I should have more friends and do more things. Besides, she likes parties an awful lot herself. It must be hard for her to imagine some-one *not* liking something she enjoys so much. I tried to imagine not liking Star and Lucy. I couldn't. So there you are.

—I guess I'm more like Daddy. He's not crazy about parties or having to give talks or having people look at him. But he's not as bad about it as I am.

Sometimes I wish I had a brother or sister. Then

maybe a little of Mom's worrying would bounce off me onto another kid.

"Did *you* have a good time, Wendy?" asked Mom. She was determined to hear one of us say the party had been fun.

Wendy wasn't fooled. She knows all about Mom and me and this party thing. She didn't want to do anything that would make me look bad. So she didn't say whether she had had a good time. Instead she said, "There was this magician at the party, Mrs. Holland. What was his name, Sara?"

"Dr. Sorcery," I replied. "And Wendy got to be his assistant."

"Yeah," said Wendy. "I broke an egg into his top hat, only he didn't mind. It turned into a birthday cupcake for Carol. . . . I wonder if I should try that in Dad's golf hat."

"I wouldn't," I said.

"And the cake was yummy," Wendy went on.

"Oh, Mom, yeah, you should have seen it!" I cried. "Uncle John put pink frosting on it and decorated it with blue and white flowers." Uncle John is this terrific baker. The only baker I know who is more terrific is Daddy. He's Uncle John's brother.

Star woke up with a start and leaped off the couch, bounding toward the den. Lucy followed. They do that sometimes and I don't know why. It's as if a silent cat alarm clock goes off somewhere.

Daddy got up from the blue armchair and sat down where the King and Queen of Fur had been. I climbed in his lap and leaned against him, feeling his beard tickle my cheek.

For a while the four of us sat quietly. Then Mom broke the silence by saying, "So what games did you play at Carol's party?"

That did it. Now we were really treading on thin ice.

Wendy stood up. "Gosh, I have to go. See you, everybody." She escaped out the front door. I didn't blame her.

"Come over after dinner," I yelled. "Bring your Malibu Barbie. We'll make a new bathing suit for her."

"'kay," she yelled back.

"Well, did you win any prizes?" asked Mom, getting back to the awful subject without wasting a second.

"No," I said, squirming uncomfortably in Daddy's lap. He patted my hand.

"What were the games you played?" Mom asked again.

I took a deep breath. "Musical chairs, egg relay races, drop-the-clothespin-in-the-bottle, and blind man's buff."

"Did you play?" asked Mom.

"Liz," said my father quietly.

"Honey, I'm just curious." Mom looked a little hurt.

"No, I didn't play."

"Oh, Sara." Mom sighed. You'd think she'd found out I'd robbed an entire town or something.

I hung my head. Daddy wrapped my hands in his.

"What did you do while the other girls played games?" asked Mom.

I didn't say anything. I was too close to tears. It hadn't been any picnic *not* playing the games (although it was better than playing). Now I was feeling bad about it all over again.

I started to struggle out of Daddy's lap, but he held me tight. "Don't you think you're being a little hard on Sara?" he asked my mother.

"For pity's sake, Chris, all I want is for her to have some fun at these parties. It's not supposed to be torture."

"But she doesn't enjoy them," said Daddy, sounding annoyed. "Why force it?"

"Well, why can't she exert herself a little? She doesn't make any effort. She spends half her time up in her room doing who knows what—"

"She's very creative," Daddy said loudly. "Who

says she has to be with people all the time?"

"It's not normal," exploded Mom.

Not normal? I wasn't normal? Mom and Daddy were talking about me like I wasn't even there. No, scratch that. They weren't talking about me; they were fighting about me. Again.

"Shut up!" I yelled, twisting off of Daddy's lap.

"Sara!" exclaimed my father. "You may not speak to us like that."

And you can't tell me I'm not normal, I wanted to say.

For a few seconds we all just stared at each other. Finally Daddy said, "Look, it's almost dinnertime. What do you say we take Hugh and go to Burger King?"

Hugh is our Volkswagen.

Mom smiled and appeared to relax. Her face softened. "Sara?" she asked me.

"Okay," I said, feeling a tiny bit better. I mean, I really love Whoppers. But a Whopper doesn't exactly make up for what just happened here. And as we bumped along in Hugh a few minutes later, I only halfway forgot about not being normal.

3.

Six Hundred and Forty Eyes

It was on Tuesday, three days after Carol's party, that the most horrible thing in the world happened. Wendy and I were sitting in the back of Mrs. Fischer's classroom passing notes as carefully as we could. We were really hot and bored. I kept looking from the thermometer to the clock. The thermometer said ninety-one degrees and the clock said 2:05.

Ninety-one degrees at 2:05 on Tuesday, May 29, in 4–B, Mrs. Fischer's fourth-grade class, in Riverside Elementary School, Riverside, New Jersey, U.S.A., North America, Earth. . . .

Poor Mrs. Fischer. It wasn't her fault we weren't paying attention. Who can concentrate on fractions when the thermometer reads ninety-one degrees? I wondered if Carol was hot and bored in 4–A, and if her teacher was making her class learn fractions, too.

"Ssst," whispered Wendy under her breath. She leaned down to the floor, supposedly to pick up her blue owl eraser.

I glanced at her and dropped my hand to my side as she straightened up. My fingers closed over a wadded-up piece of notebook paper. Staring straight ahead at Mrs. Fischer, I opened the paper inside my desk. The paper was all creased and soft from being passed so much. It hardly made a sound as I unfolded it.

Mrs. Fischer turned her back to put a new problem on the board, and I peeked at the note. It said: *Mrs. Fischer's bra strap is showing.*

I looked up at Mrs. Fischer. Sure enough, the shoulder strap was sticking out past her sleeveless blouse.

I started to giggle silently, which is sometimes very hard to do. I was in danger of snorting. I forced myself to calm down.

I felt a little bad about laughing, anyway. First of all, Wendy and I don't usually fool around in class. Fourth grade was the first time we'd been in the same classroom since Wendy's family moved to Riverside the summer before second grade. So all this year we'd wanted to giggle and pass notes and draw pictures, but we tried to keep a lid on it. We felt lucky just to be allowed to sit next to each other in the back row.

The other reason I felt guilty about laughing at Mrs. Fischer's bra strap is that I really like Mrs. Fischer. She's my all-time favorite teacher. Mom says she's been good for me. I guess she has. All I know is that this is the first year I've liked school. I think Wendy has something to do with that, too, though. She makes everything easier for me.

I don't like many things about school—for instance, oral reports, reading aloud, talking in class, group projects, and especially *gym*. But with Wendy around, things are different. When Mrs. Fischer calls on me, Wendy looks at me and smiles. Then I feel better. In gym, Wendy chooses me to be on her team. She never throws the ball at me in dodgeball, and sometimes in baseball she covers for me. She says it's good practice for her. We always try to be in the outfield together. I pay her back by showing her how to do lots of things—make doll clothes, draw horses, string beaded jewelry. Those are the things I'm good at and Wendy's not so good at. Once, I got this idea for making lots of stuff and selling it at a sidewalk stand. Wendy and Carol thought it would be fun, so they pitched in. We made $4.83 each.

Anyway, back to school. This year's been pretty good. Wendy and I teamed up for the social studies project. We made a stained-glass window. We copied a picture of a window that's in a big church in Paris. I figured out how to glue the colored tissue paper to make it look like stained glass. Wendy read our report while I stood next to her in front of the class and held up the window. Wendy didn't mind doing the reading, and we got an A on our project. We still have the window, too. It spends a week in my bedroom, a week in Wendy's, and so on. Only now there's a hole in an angel's ear where Wendy's sister poked it accidentally.

Suddenly I realized everybody was closing their math books. School was almost over for another day. Mrs. Fischer would give us our homework assignments, and then we'd be free until tomorrow.

I got out my Snoopy assignment book and turned to a blank page. I waited for Mrs. Fischer to start writing on the blackboard. Instead she walked over to her desk and picked up a huge pile of white booklets. She carried them to a table in the front of the room.

My heart began to beat a little faster. A change. This could be very good—or very bad.

I glanced at Wendy. She looked back at me and shrugged.

Mrs. Fischer divided the booklets into three piles. Then she asked Sandy Murphy, Joy Benton, and Bob Mulligan to pass them out. When Joy handed me the first one, I opened it gingerly, as if something might spring out at me. I looked at the first page. It read:

THE DOG WHO WOULDN'T BEHAVE
A Play

A *play*. Oh, no, no, no.

Then Bob ran by my desk and slung another booklet on it. This one said:

UNCLE ELMER'S FABULOUS IDEA
A Play

Another play. The third booklet was a play, too, of course. It was called "The Haunted Cave Mystery." I began to feel very nervous.

All the kids—except me—were looking through the play booklets and talking excitedly. Mrs. Fischer flicked the overhead lights for quiet. When she had our attention, she said, "Class, I want to tell you about our special end-of-the-year project. We're going to put on a play, which we'll perform in the June Festival for our families. Sandy, Joy, and Bob have just passed out the scripts for three different plays. Your assignment tonight is to read the scripts— they're very short. Tomorrow we can vote on which

one to perform. Is that clear?"

Oh, boy, was it ever. Why was she doing this? This was worse than playing games at parties, worse than giving oral reports, even worse than gym. I was dying. I was really dying.

Suddenly everyone had a million questions.

"What's the June Festival?" asked Bob, who was new at Riverside this year.

"It's an evening program given during the last week of the school year," said Mrs. Fischer. "Any class can participate. There's usually singing and choral speaking and a couple of skits or plays. Sometimes one of the classes gives a recorder recital."

Bob nodded his head.

"How many parts are in these plays?" asked Wendy, waving her scripts.

"Each has enough parts for every student in the class. That's one reason I chose these particular plays," explained Mrs. Fischer. "I want all of you to have the experience of performing."

Mrs. Fischer went on talking, but I didn't hear another word. I'd heard enough already. More than enough.

I really, really thought I was going to faint. Or barf.

How could I perform in a play when I couldn't even talk in class? In Mrs. Fischer's class, exactly forty-two eyes (not counting Mrs. Fischer's) watch you when you have to answer a question. How many eyes would be watching me during the June Festival? Let's see, our auditorium can hold about three hundred people. That's six hundred eyes. If extra people came and stood in the aisles, that could be six hundred thirty or six hundred forty eyes.

What was I going to do? What on *earth* was I going to do?

Mrs. Fischer was not my favorite teacher anymore. In fact, she had suddenly become the Witch of Riverside School.

4.

Wendy's Disaster

"Wendy!" I called, dashing down our front steps. "Hi!" I ran across the lawn, jumping over Star, who was rolling in the grass. I shouted goodbye to Mom and Daddy. They were watching me from the front door. They do that every morning. It makes me feel safe.

Wendy was waiting for me on the sidewalk. She was carrying her blue book bag with the apple on it, and her Smurfs lunch box.

I had my "I ♡ Cats" book bag and a Garfield lunch box.

It was Wednesday morning. After this week we had only three more weeks of school. Then we were free, free, free! For seventy-three lazy summer days.

Usually at this time of year I'm so happy I could

burst, but the thought of the play had dampened my spirits. A lot.

"Well?" I asked Wendy as we started off down the sidewalk. Sometimes we walk with Carol, but she's almost always late. We ended up leaving without her.

"Well what?" said Wendy. She sounded grumpy.

"Well, did you read the plays?" The plays were all I could think about.

"Oh, yeah."

Somehow I'd thought Wendy would be more excited. She loves being onstage or giving concerts or recitals. Not like me. I remembered last night when I'd taken the plays out of my book bag. I'd spread them across the bed and stared at them, hating them. At first I'd decided not to read them, but then I'd gotten an idea. I looked through them very carefully. I found out that "Uncle Elmer's Fabulous Idea" was five whole pages shorter than "The Dog Who Wouldn't Behave" and six and a half pages shorter than "The Haunted Cave Mystery." It had more small parts, too. I was glad I'd checked them out.

"Which one are you going to vote for?" I asked.

"One what?"

"Wendy!"

"What?"

She looked at me as if she'd just woken up.

"Come *on*," I said. "You're not listening. Which play do you want to put on? What's wrong with you today?"

"We're moving," she said flatly.

For several seconds I felt numb. Then I giggled. It must be a joke. "Oh, Wendy," I said. She was trying to make me forget about the play.

Wendy glared at me. "Quit laughing," she said crossly. "It's not funny. You wouldn't be laughing if *you* were moving."

"You mean it's true?" This was more horrible than the play.

"Of course it's true. Dad told us last night. He came home from work in a rotten mood and said his boss wants to transfer him to Chicago to start some new project."

"Oh, *no* . . ."

"Yeah. The only thing is, Mom doesn't want to leave *her* job." Wendy's mother is a lawyer. "She says she has her clients to think about. So Dad's going to look for another job around here."

I started to let out a sigh of relief.

"*But*," said Wendy, before I could feel too relieved, "if he can't find one, we'll have to move. Mom said that even though she'd rather stay here, she can find clients in any town."

I nodded. I couldn't say another word. If we hadn't

been so close to school, I would have cried.

What would I *do* without Wendy? Who would I make Malibu Barbie doll clothes with? Who would choose me to be on her team in gym? Who would I spend the summer days with? Who would rescue me in school before I even knew I needed rescuing?

Oh, Carol would be around, of course, but it wasn't the same.

It just wasn't the same.

The only good thing about Wendy's disaster was that it kept my mind off the play. She broke the news to Carol in the cafeteria at lunchtime. That was all we talked about.

"I can't believe it," said Wendy as she bit into her pizzaburger. "Dad *promised* when we moved here that it would be our last move. We've only lived in Riverside for two and three-quarter years. That's the longest I've lived anywhere. Before that, Dad's company moved us once a year. I went to two different nursery schools, another school for kindergarten, and another for first grade. Then Dad said enough was enough. No more moving. I thought he meant it."

"Maybe he did but his boss didn't," suggested Carol.

"Maybe," said Wendy unhappily. "Still . . ."

"It's not fair," I said firmly.

Wendy and Carol shook their heads in agreement.

"If you have to move, when will it be?" I asked.

"I don't know. This summer, I guess," answered Wendy. "Dad always scheduled our moves for the summer so Katie and Scott and I wouldn't have to switch schools in the middle of the year."

"This summer!" I yelped. "That's practically right *now!*"

"Yeah!" cried Carol.

"Don't remind me," muttered Wendy.

We went back to our pizzaburgers. I finished mine and picked through my salad. I put all the pieces of celery under the pizzaburger crusts, then ate the carrots, and then the radishes. I left the lettuce in a big, soggy pile.

Nobody was talking. Wendy picked at her fruit Jell-O and Carol picked at her apple crisp.

"Well, this is just dumb," I announced finally.

Carol and Wendy looked at me in surprise.

"Wendy might not even move, right?"

They nodded.

"So let's forget about it for a while. Let's go outside and work on the Barbie poem." Wendy and Carol and I are writing a poem about Barbie and Ken and their children and their lives. It's called "The Saga of Barbie and Ken," and it's the world's longest poem written by kids. So far it has three hundred and twenty-two stanzas. We're going to send it to *The Guinness Book of World Records*.

So we left the cafeteria and sat under the spreading oak tree with our pads and pencils. We sat under the oak tree because it's at the far end of the playground where the boys wouldn't bother us. We wrote until recess was over. When the bell rang, we'd added four stanzas to the saga. Now it was three hundred and twenty-six stanzas long. We were going to wait until we hit four hundred stanzas before we sent it to *The Guinness Book*.

As we were lining up to go back to our classroom, my stomach began to feel funny. I wished I hadn't eaten so much pizzaburger.

"Wendy," I said, "I don't feel too good."

"What's the matter? You felt okay while we were writing the poem."

"I don't know. It's my stomach. Maybe I better go to the nurse."

"You have to tell Mrs. Fischer first. Come on back to the classroom."

Wendy put her arm around me and walked me down the long hall to 4–B.

"Mrs. Fischer," she said importantly as she steered me toward her desk, "Sara doesn't feel well. I'm going to take her to the nurse, okay?"

"What's wrong, Sara?" asked Mrs. Fischer, putting her hand on my forehead.

"I feel sick to my stomach." Sometimes Mrs. Fischer believes that and sometimes she doesn't. Kids say they feel sick to their stomachs a lot.

Mrs. Fischer looked closely at me. "Your cheeks are nice and pink," she said. "We're just about to vote on the play, and I'd like your vote. Why don't you wait here awhile and see how you feel?"

"All right," I said reluctantly. I didn't feel all that bad, but I didn't feel wonderful, either.

Wendy and I went to our seats, and the class quieted down.

"Okay," began Mrs. Fischer, "has everyone read the plays? Raise your hand if you have."

We all raised our hands except for Stacey Montgomery, who'd been absent yesterday.

"Good," said Mrs. Fischer. "Now we're going to choose the play to perform in the June Festival. Before we vote, I want you to take a few more minutes to look through the plays and think about the following things."

She wrote on the blackboard:

Which play has a part you would most like
    to perform?
Which play will be most enjoyed by both

children and adults (your audience)?

For which play would you most like to
make scenery and costumes?

Which play did you most enjoy reading?

I didn't even think about Mrs. Fischer's questions.
I was voting for "Uncle Elmer" no matter what. We
just *had* to choose it. It was my best chance at getting
a teensy-weensy part.

At last Mrs. Fischer said, "Okay, class. Please put
your heads down on your desks. I'll call out the name
of each play. When you hear the play you'd like us
to perform, raise your hand. You may vote only
once."

I buried my head in my arms and breathed in the
smell of pencils and erasers and wood. My breath
steamed up the desktop, and my stomach did flip-
flops.

"'The Dog Who Wouldn't Behave,'" called out
Mrs. Fischer.

I listened to the rustles around me, and could tell
Wendy had just voted.

"'Uncle Elmer's Fabulous Idea.'"

I waved my hand frantically.

"'The Haunted Cave Mystery.'"

More rustlings.

"Okay, class. Heads up."

We lifted our heads, blinking our eyes in the light.

"Here are the results," said Mrs. Fischer.

I held my breath.

"'The Dog Who Wouldn't Behave'—five. 'Uncle Elmer'—ten. 'The Haunted Cave'—seven."

"Yay!" cheered ten voices. One of them was mine. I was actually cheering. What a relief. I almost forgot that I still had to be *in* the play.

Our homework assignment that night was to read "Uncle Elmer" again. We had to decide which part we'd each like to play, and rehearse it.

Auditions were tomorrow.

Boo.

5.

No Deal

Brrrring! Slam, slam. Clatter. Scrape.

The bell rang, and school was over for another day. All around me, kids gathered up their notebooks and pencils and book bags and knapsacks.

Wendy stood by my desk waiting.

"You go ahead," I told her. "I'll see you later." I had an idea. I needed to talk to Mrs. Fischer about it.

Wendy looked like she wanted to ask me a question. Instead, she said quietly, "Okay, Sara," and left 4–B.

I sat at my desk and watched Mrs. Fischer's back as she erased the blackboard (which was really a greenboard).

When she finished, she turned around. "Sara!"

she exclaimed. "You gave me a fright. I didn't know anyone was still here."

"Sorry," I said. I hadn't meant to scare Mrs. Fischer. I sure wasn't off to a very good start.

"Is anything wrong?"

"I . . . no. I—I was just wondering. Could I talk to you about something?"

"The play?" asked Mrs. Fischer.

Now, how did she know that? "Yes," I said. I decided to be very firm about this. "Mrs. Fischer," I began, "I would rather not be in the play. I don't like being the center of attention. I don't even like people looking at me. But the thing is, I'm really good at art. If you let me out of the play, I'll design the costumes or some of the scenery instead. I'll write a report about designing costumes and scenery, too. I'll work really hard. I promise. I'll—"

"Sara," Mrs. Fischer broke in, "I know you'd do a good job on a project like that. You're a smart girl and a hard worker. But I want you—and the rest of the students—to have a new experience. Most of you have never had the opportunity to perform—"

"But I don't *want* to perform, Mrs. Fischer. I *can't* perform."

"You usually don't want to do your spelling homework, either. But you do it, and do it well."

"I won't perform well," I said.

"So you won't perform well, Sara. That's okay. You don't do *every*thing well. You're much better in science than in social studies. And you're terrific in art, but not so hot in gym. Everyone is good at some things and poor at some things. Besides, you will get to work on the costumes and scenery. The class will make those together, as part of the project."

"But what about . . . what about the lights? And the sound effects? Who will take care of those while we're putting the play on?" I had Mrs. Fischer on *that* one, I thought.

"Our class will plan them, and some of the students in Mr. Howell's class will handle them during the performance for extra credit," replied Mrs. Fischer.

I was running out of excuses. What else could I say? I'd thought for sure she'd agree to my bargain. I looked at my shoes. "What about—" I started to say.

"Sara, I'm afraid the subject is closed. I can't make an exception for you. If I did, I'd have to make exceptions for other students. I understand that you're shy and that performing will be difficult. I also think it will be a very good experience for you. I believe you'll do a better job than you think you will. And maybe I can help you get over some of your stage fright. . . . Okay?"

Stage fright. So that was what I had.

Slowly, I picked up my notebook and slid it into my book bag. "Okay," I said. I could feel a lump forming in my throat. I stood up quickly.

"'Bye," I whispered, and fled from the classroom.

"Sara," I heard Mrs. Fischer call, but I didn't stop. When I reached the main entrance to Riverside Elementary School, I paused inside the doorway. I leaned against the wall, taking deep breaths. When I felt calm, I walked outside.

"BOO!" shrieked a shrill voice.

"Yikes!" I bet I jumped a mile. "Wendy White! Don't you ever do that again!" I cried. But I was giggling. I couldn't help it.

"BOO!" shrieked another voice, just as I was getting calm again.

"*Carol!*" I yelled, and chased her down the steps. Wendy followed us. We collapsed under an elm tree and laughed until we couldn't laugh anymore.

"You *guys*," I said, sitting up.

"We wanted to wait for you," said Wendy. "Let's walk home together."

"Okay," I said. I knew Wendy wanted to hear why I'd stayed after school. But I didn't feel like talking about it.

For a while nobody said anything. We didn't want to talk about Wendy moving, either.

As we turned the corner onto Overbrook Drive,

Wendy said, "I know! Let's rehearse the play at my house."

I groaned.

"Oh, come on, Sara. We've got to rehearse for the auditions. We might as well do it together."

"Can I come, too?"asked Carol. "I could read some parts."

"Sure," said Wendy. "That'd be great. Right, Sara?"

"Right," I agreed half-heartedly. But maybe it wouldn't be so bad with just Carol and Wendy.

We reached our houses, and Carol ran inside to dump off her books and tell Aunt Martha she'd be at Wendy's. I ran up my front lawn and found Mom weeding the myrtle bed, with Star and Lucy at her side.

"Hi," I said. "I'm going over to Wendy's."

I pulled my play booklet out of my book bag, tossed the bag onto the bench inside the front door, and dashed back out.

"Don't you want to change your clothes?" Mom called after me.

"No," I called back.

Carol and I got to Wendy's front porch at the same time and let ourselves in. The three of us go in and out of each other's houses without even ringing doorbells.

We found Wendy in the kitchen with the Whites'

housekeeper, Miss Johnson, and Scott and Katie. Katie was wearing these space cadet boots. They were the big thing in her third-grade classroom then. She'd been leaping around in them for a week.

"Hi!" she cried, bouncing over to us.

"Hi!" cried Scott, running up behind her. Scott is five and doesn't like to be left out of anything.

"Hi," Carol and I said back.

Miss Johnson turned away from the stove where she'd been stirring something in a pot. "How are you girls?" she asked warmly. "Would you like a snack? There's some squash bread in the fridge."

Miss Johnson is into health food. Wendy, Katie, and Scott are the healthiest kids I've ever seen in my life.

Carol and I helped ourselves to slices of squash bread. I could use a little health. I'd be needing my strength for the play.

We sat around the Whites' big table and munched away. Then we went upstairs. Katie and Scott followed us.

"Out, you guys!" ordered Wendy when Katie and Scott tried to come into her room.

"What are you going to do?" whined Katie.

"Rehearse," said Wendy. "And don't whine."

"I want to rehearse with you," wailed Katie.

"Me, too," said Scott.

"Out," cried Wendy again, trying to close the door against Katie. "We need our privacy."

"I'm telling!" yelled Katie, and charged back downstairs.

"Me, too," yelled Scott.

"It's okay," Wendy assured us. "Miss Johnson knows we have to work."

Wendy and Carol and I sat on Wendy's bed and looked at the play booklets. Carol and I shared mine.

"All right," said Wendy, taking charge. "Let's try the first scene. Carol, you be Tom the Ragman, Sara, you be Aunt Baldy, and I'll be Uncle Elmer and also Fido."

We started our rehearsal. We read the scene four times. When we'd gotten the hang of it, we read the whole play from beginning to end, each taking about a million parts.

"Gosh, you're *good*, Sara!" exclaimed Wendy when we were finished.

Good? Me? Well, it was true, the reading wasn't as bad as I'd thought it would be. In fact, it was fun. Sort of. Of course, tomorrow would be another story. Tomorrow forty-two eyes would be watching me.

6.

Tryouts

But Barbie and Ken,
they never did think,
that old Hostess Twinkies,
would clog up their sink.
So they called the man
from Roto-Rooter,
who came to their house
on a blue moto-scooter.
And he cleaned up the mess,
and saved the day,
and bid them adieu
as he roared away.

That was stanza #329 in "The Saga of Barbie and Ken." We knew there was no such thing as a moto-scooter, but it rhymed exactly with Roto-Rooter.

Wendy said there was something called poetic license and that we should take advantage of it.

It was Thursday, the day of the tryouts. Carol and Wendy and I were sitting under our tree on the playground. We were trying to squeeze out the three hundred and thirtieth stanza of the saga before recess was over.

We probably weren't going to make it, though. I was having too much trouble concentrating. That was because the tryouts were coming up right after recess.

I leaned back against the tree trunk and thought.

"Wendy?" I asked.

"Yeah?"

"Did your dad say anything about his job?"

"No."

Wendy didn't want to talk about it at all.

The bell rang.

"Nuts," said Carol. "We didn't make it. Only three hundred and twenty-nine. Oh, well."

We gathered up our stuff and got in line.

This is it, I thought. The beginning of the end.

We filed into our classrooms. Wendy and I said goodbye to Carol.

As soon as we sat down, Mrs. Fischer started in on the tryouts. You could tell she was really excited about them.

"Okay," she began, clapping her hands for silence. "The biggest parts in the play are Uncle Elmer, Aunt Baldy, Fido, and Tom the Ragman. We'll hold those tryouts first. Who would like to read for the part of Uncle Elmer?"

Four hands shot up. One of them was Wendy's.

"Wendy!" I hissed. "You can't be Uncle Elmer. You're a *girl!*"

"So what?" said Wendy. "This is a play. It's all make-believe."

I grinned.

Mrs. Fischer called Wendy, Andy Chase, Bob Mulligan, and Brett Miles to the front of the room. "Open your play books to page six," she said. "I'd like each of you to read Uncle Elmer's part in the scene with Aunt Baldy. I'll be Aunt Baldy for now."

The scene on page six was a really important one to the play. See, "Uncle Elmer's Fabulous Idea" is a story about a man named Uncle Elmer who's very poor and lives on the edge of a little town with his mean wife, Aunt Baldy. He thinks he should get Fido, a lost dog, and Tom, a lonely old rag collector, together so they can keep each other company. But first he has to convince Tom he needs Fido. Then he has to figure out how to stand up to Aunt Baldy, who is pushy and awful. The characters in the play are the four main ones, five medium-sized ones—

Elmer and Baldy's nieces and nephews—and a lot of little parts for some townspeople. Mostly they just yell at Aunt Baldy and shout encouragement to Tom and Uncle Elmer in the last act.

Page six was where Elmer gets his fabulous idea and tells it to Baldy. Then she starts yelling and carrying on about how Elmer shouldn't stick his nose in other people's business.

Brett got to read first. He was okay because he put a lot of expression into his reading, but it sounded funny because he talks with a lisp:

> UNCLE ELMER: Lishen to thish fabuloush idea, Baldy.
>
> AUNT BALDY: Elmer, none of your ideas has ever been fabulous.
>
> UNCLE ELMER: Well, thish one ish. It'sh shuper fabuloush. It'sh shplendiferoush. It'sh—
>
> AUNT BALDY: Can it!

Everyone giggled. It sounded as if Mrs. Fischer meant for Brett to can it.

Bob read next. He was terrible. He sounded like a record going at high speed:

> UNCLE ELMER: Listentothisfabulousidea-Baldy.
>
> AUNT BALDY: Elmer, none of your ideas has

ever been fabulous.

UNCLE ELMER:

Wellthisoneisit'ssuperfabu-
lousit'ssplendiferousit's—

AUNT BALDY: Can it!

Everybody giggled again. I sure wouldn't have wanted to be Bob right then.

Wendy got to read after Bob. She was great. She didn't speak too fast or too slow, and she read with feeling. The only thing was, she waved her hands around an awful lot.

"Listen to this *fabulous* idea, Baldy!" she cried, sweeping her arms open wide. To show just how fabulous the idea was, I guess.

And, "It's *splendiferous!*" she shouted, raising her arms and tossing her head back.

"Can it!"

I was the first one to giggle.

After Andy read for Elmer's part, Mrs. Fischer told the four Uncle Elmers to take their seats. She didn't say who had gotten the part.

Instead she asked who wanted to try out for the part of Aunt Baldy. When those auditions were over, she tried out kids for Fido and for Tom the Ragman. Wendy tried out for every part. I didn't raise my hand once. I wasn't the only one, though. There were a few others. I kept watching Jennifer Sarason, who was sitting in front of me. She was sliding lower and lower in her chair. I knew just how she felt.

Next came the auditions for the nieces and nephews. They didn't take long. Mrs. Fischer asked them all to read the same paragraph.

When that was over, I looked at the clock. Two-fifteen! Maybe we wouldn't have time for any more auditions. Maybe—

"Joy, Chip, Jennifer, Sara, and Randall, please come to the front of the room. Bring your play books."

Me? *Me?* What was she calling on *me* for? My hand wasn't raised. It hardly ever is.

I could feel my legs turning to spaghetti. I watched Joy, Chip, Jennifer, and Randall stand up and walk to the front. They looked like they were moving in slow motion. We were not a great group. We were the Deadbeats of 4–B.

"Sara," Mrs. Fischer called again.

I managed to get to my feet. Then I managed to find my way up to the blackboard. My legs had turned from spaghetti to Jell-O. I stood absolutely still. I stared at the floor, silently telling the Jell-O not to give out under me.

"You five will be reading for the parts of the townspeople," announced Mrs. Fischer. "Please open

your booklets to page nineteen."

My hands were shaking so hard I could barely turn the pages. They were sweating, too. My hands, that is. Not the pages.

"Sara," said Mrs. Fischer, "please take the part of Polly Esther. I want you to read the line at the top of the page."

Why me? *Why me?*

I looked at the line. It read: *GO FOR IT, UNCLE ELMER!*

I had a feeling it was supposed to be shouted. Okay, Mrs. Fischer, I'll try my worst. Then maybe you'll change your mind and let me make scenery instead.

"GoforitUncleElmer," I whispered.

"Sara," said Mrs. Fischer, "that line is so loud it's practically jumping off the page. Please put some feeling into it."

The Jell-O was turning to water. I glanced across the room at all the eyes on me, and found Wendy's. She crossed them at me.

I felt a teeny bit better.

"Go for it, Uncle Elmel!" I said, a smidgen louder. I was torn. I wanted to sound terrible so I wouldn't get the part, but if I improved the line right this second, maybe Mrs. Fischer would let me sit down.

"Please try again, Sara."

Again?

"Go for it, Uncker Elmel!" I said loudly.

Everyone laughed.

I blushed fire-engine red. But I knew I'd done a pretty bad job. There was no way Mrs. Fischer could want me in her play.

Mrs. Fischer sighed. "Okay. Thank you, Sara."

Chip read next. He was about as bad and as quiet as I'd been. He even threw in a few nervous stutters: "H-H-Hurray f-f-for Uncle El-muh-mer," he mumbled. The class needed a giant hearing aid to hear him.

I was trying to hear Chip when I realized that Jennifer Sarason, who was standing near me, was crying. *Crying.* She was very quiet about it, but she was crying, all right. She kept brushing away tears and wiping her eyes and gulping in air. I couldn't believe it. She was in worse shape than I was.

Mrs. Fischer finished with Joy and Randall and looked at Jennifer. With a quick, sidelong glance at me, she said, "Jen, do you want to read?"

Well, of all the stupid questions!

Jennifer shook her head, wiping her eyes. Suddenly I squeezed her hand. I felt as if she needed to be taken care of.

Mrs. Fischer nodded briskly. "All right," she said. She faced the class. "Okay, people, auditions are over."

"But Jennifer didn't—" someone started to say.

Mrs. Fischer kept right on talking, as if she hadn't heard the interruption. "On Monday, I'll announce the parts I've assigned to each of you. Thank you for your hard work. You've tried your best, and I think 4–B is going to put on one terrific play."

The bell rang then. It sounded like a period at the end of her speech.

I let out a huge breath. I had survived auditions.

That afternoon, I curled up on the couch with Star and Lucy and watched rain dripping down the bay window in our living room. A thunderstorm had blown up on the way home from school, and now it had settled into a steady drizzle. The air felt cold and damp, but Star and Lucy were warm. I lay next to them with my feet propped up on the back of the couch. I told them about auditioning.

"It was horrible," I said, petting them both at the same time, "really horrible."

Star purred loudly.

Lucy rolled over on her back and put her front paws on my chin.

"I had to stand up in front of all those eyes and read aloud. With feeling. I was supposed to shout, but I couldn't work up a good one. . . . You guys are lucky. You couldn't shout if you tried."

Star swished his tail across Lucy's face, and she

batted at it. They were waking up.

"Pay attention!" I scolded them.

Lucy's tail twitched warningly.

"Well, anyway," I went on, "just be glad *you'll* never have to audition for anything. I wouldn't make you do it. Not even for a cat food commercial. . . . The kids laughed at me. I was hoping I wouldn't have to audition at all. Then when my turn came, I did my worst. I bet Mrs. Fischer won't want me in her old play now after—"

"Sara!" exclaimed my mother suddenly.

She barged around the corner into the living room. She didn't sound too happy. "*What* did you do?"

"What?" I asked, feeling frightened. I swung my feet quickly to the floor. Mom could be upset with me about any number of things: feet on the couch, talking to the Cat Kids, being alone, wasting time.

"Did I hear you say you tried your *worst* so Mrs. Fischer wouldn't want you in the play?"

Uh-oh. I must have been talking louder than I thought. Mom knew all about the play, of course, and knew how I felt about it. This morning she'd given me a big pep talk. It was about how good the play would be for me, and how much I should enjoy it. Then she'd said, "Promise me you'll try hard and get a good part so I can be proud of you." And I'd promised. What else could I have done?

Now I didn't know what to tell Mom to make things better. I was already in trouble. Big trouble.

"Did you do that?" Mom repeated, her face growing pink.

"Yes," I mumbled.

"What? I can't hear you."

"Yes. I did do that."

"Sara Holland, I'm amazed at you. I really am. I'm ashamed of you, too. What gets into you sometimes? Do you know that not trying your best is the same as *cheating?*"

I shrank back against the couch cushions and reached for one of the Cat People. They'd left the scene. They never hang around long when voices are raised.

"Did you hear me?"

"Yes, yes."

"And?"

"I don't know, Mom. It's . . . I just can't . . . all those people . . ."

"For heaven's sake, Sara. All *what* people? They're your friends."

"You don't under—" I started to say, and stopped. It was not a good idea to tell Mom she didn't understand. It made her mad. But I was too late.

"I don't understand?" she asked, blinking her eyes.

"I guess not. Believe me, Sara, if you were a few years younger I'd turn you over my knee and spank you. I can't tell you how ashamed I am. I expect more from you than this."

She paused. I guessed she expected something *else* from me, but I wasn't sure what.

She frowned. "Go to your room," she said at last. "Stay there until dinner."

I went.

It's funny, I thought as I lay on my bed cuddling Star. (It turned out the Cat People had fled to my room.) Mom complains that I spend too much time alone in my room, yet what does she do to punish me? She sends me to be alone in my room. It's kind of like punishing someone by giving him an ice-cream cone.

An hour or so later, I heard muffled voices downstairs. Daddy was home.

The voices droned on awhile. Then they grew louder. I crept to the top of the stairs and listened.

Same old thing.

"You know how she feels about being in the play," said Daddy, sounding tired and cross. "You're asking her to do the last thing in the world she wants to do. And you're asking her to do *well* at it. Not only that, to enjoy it. That's crazy."

"Crazy!" exploded Mom.

I didn't need to hear any more. I tiptoed back to my room and closed my door.

But I could still hear their voices.

7.

Playing Nellie

On Monday, just as she had promised, Mrs. Fischer assigned the parts in the play. Wendy and I had come in from recess and sat down at our desks. I was feeling pretty happy. We had just written three more stanzas in the saga. Barbie was going to have another baby, and she and Ken were very excited. We decided Barbie and Ken should have seventeen children in all—two sets of triplets, three sets of twins, and five regular kids.

I was so pleased at how long the saga was growing that I was hardly nervous about the play. I knew I'd have to be in it no matter what, but I also knew I'd only get one of those teensy-weensy two-line parts. Anyone who blushed and mumbled and said "Uncker Elmel" wouldn't get a big part.

I sat smugly at my desk. All in all, I was pretty pleased with myself.

Mrs. Fischer flicked the lights and waited for silence.

At last she took a piece of paper from her desk. "Class," she said, "I've made my decisions about the cast for 'Uncle Elmer's Fabulous Idea.' It wasn't easy. You were all very good. . . ." (She paused here and I knew she was telling a big fat lie.) "I hope nobody will be too disappointed. These are my final choices, and there will not be any switching of parts. The part I've assigned you is the part you'll play. Do you understand?"

We nodded.

"Good. I'll announce the four main parts first."

I didn't pay too much attention to those, except to hear what Wendy got. When Mrs. Fischer said, "The part of Aunt Baldy will be played by Wendy White," Wendy just smiled. It wasn't a big smile. I knew she wanted to be Uncle Elmer. But Andy Chase had gotten that part. Besides, Wendy really had given the best reading for Baldy. If she could stop waving her hands around, she'd be terrific.

"Now," continued Mrs. Fischer, "I'll announce the parts of the five nieces and nephews."

I had just started to drift off into a nice daydream about Barbie's and Ken's seventeenth kid when I heard Mrs. Fischer say, "And the part of Nellie, the third niece, will be played by Sara Holland."

I sat bolt upright. I felt as if I'd walked into an electric fence.

What had she said?

I couldn't have heard right.

I looked over at Wendy. She was staring at me, wide-eyed, as surprised as I was.

Something was wrong. When Mrs. Fischer announced the smallest parts — the parts of the thirteen townspeople — I listened very carefully. My name would be in there somewhere. I'd just been day-dreaming before and misunderstood her.

But my name wasn't in there.

Jennifer Sarason's was, though. The lucky stiff. Maybe I should have cried, too.

Somehow I made it to the end of the afternoon. When the bell rang, I closed my notebook. I pulled my books out of the desk and loaded everything into my bag. I was a robot, moving mechanically.

"Sara, may I see you for a minute, please?" Mrs. Fischer caught my arm as I filed by her.

I dropped onto the nearest chair.

When the rest of the kids had left, Mrs. Fischer said to me, "I think you can handle the part of Nellie. I really do. And I'll be glad to help you with your stage fright. You can overcome it. Lots of famous actors and actresses have overcome stage fright."

I nodded dumbly. I didn't know what to say. Finally I just left the classroom.

If Mrs. Fischer wanted me to ruin her dumb play, that was her business.

Wendy asked me to come over after school that afternoon, but all I felt like doing was curling up in my room with Star and Lucy. I hauled Looz onto my lap and put old Starbo next to me. Then I patted them and told them a story.

After a while I knew I was going to have to do what I'd been dreading.

I was going to have to see how many lines Nellie had.

With shaking hands, I drew the play book out of my book bag.

I scanned Act I. Aunt Baldy, Uncle Elmer, Tom the Ragman, and Fido were the only characters in the whole act.

What a relief. One down, two to go.

I turned the page to Act II.

Act II opened with the nieces and nephews sitting around the table in Baldy's and Elmer's kitchen. Uncle Elmer was telling them about Tom and Fido.

Nellie's first line is, "Did you talk to Tom, Uncle

Elmer?" Later, when one of the nephews pinches her, Nellie is supposed to say, "Cut it out, Truman!" and sound angry. At the end of the scene, I would have to get up from my chair and walk to Uncle Elmer. Then I was supposed to put my hand on his shoulder (it would really be yucky Andy's gross shoulder) and say, "*I* think it's a *won*derful idea, Uncle!" I could tell it was supposed to be said with feeling. I'd see about that.

This wasn't terrific.

I turned to Act III, the act in which all the townspeople and the nieces and nephews gather on Main Street, shouting at Elmer and Baldy and Tom. First I'd have to whisper loudly to Rose, the townsperson standing next to me, "Tom's an old fool if he won't listen to my uncle." (Rose, by the way, would be Jennifer Sarason.) My last line, "Listen to him, Tom," was supposed to be said "urgently and with feeling."

Ha.

I slammed the play book shut.

Darn old Mrs. Fischer.

The very next day, rehearsals began. All that week during English period, we broke into little groups. We were supposed to help each other memorize our lines.

Wendy and I made sure we were always in the same group.

"Just practice saying your lines out loud," Mrs. Fischer told our class. "Pretty soon you won't need your play books. You'll be surprised at how fast it happens."

That first day, Jennifer was in a group that included Wendy, me, and Stacey Montgomery.

Jennifer cried.

I blushed and stammered and whispered.

Wendy and Stacey rolled their eyes.

Mrs. Fischer tried to look patient.

"Pretend you're just reading aloud in your reading group," she told me.

I pretended. But I didn't like reading groups any better than plays.

By the end of the week, I had my lines memorized, though.

The next week, we started rehearsing scenes in front of the classroom. Mrs. Fischer helped each of us with our problems. She wanted Jennifer and me to speak louder, and she wanted Wendy to stop waving her hands around so much. When we got to Act III with the townspeople, Jennifer sniffled, I forgot my lines, Wendy waved madly, and Mrs. Fischer put her head in her hands.

I told you so, I thought.

"Sara," she said after school that day, "you forget your lines because you're nervous and tense. Try taking deep breaths before you have to speak. It will relax you."

I tried it. I got the hiccups.

But after three days, I could say my lines right on cue, and Jennifer had stopped sniffling. Especially if I gave her a little pep talk before each rehearsal. And Wendy was trying hard to control her hands.

One afternoon, Mrs. Fischer lined us up and took us down the hall to the auditorium.

"We're going to rehearse some scenes on the stage," she said.

Forty-two eyes, forty-two eyes. That was all I could think of.

I got up on the stage to rehearse the scene in Baldy and Elmer's kitchen. I looked out at my classmates and Mrs. Fischer and the janitor and some PTA people and a couple of room mothers who had peeked in.

Every single one of my lines flew out of my head.

"Imagine the people in the audience wearing nothing but their underwear," Mrs. Fischer told me after school. "How could you be nervous in front of people in their underwear?"

But it was the eyes that bothered me, not what the bodies under the eyes were (or weren't) wearing.

I thought about asking Mrs. Fischer just one more time if she'd let me out of the play. But I couldn't think of anything for me to work on instead. In art class we were making props and scenery. We'd made a stove for Baldy to cook on during Act II, and we were painting a backdrop to look like Main Street. Everybody was collecting junk for Tom the Ragman's shack.

There were our costumes, of course, but after a class discussion, we'd decided that each person would be responsible for his or her own costume.

So there was nothing left for me to do—except be in the play.

8.

Nothing but Trouble

So Barbie and Ken
climbed into their boat,
and sailed away
past the castle moat.
"Goodbye!" they called.
"We'll see you again
when our adventures are over
and our good deeds done."

That was the last stanza in "The Saga of Barbie and Ken." We were finished. We hadn't reached #400, though. We'd gotten tired of rhyming, and we'd given up after three hundred and fifty stanzas. But we still thought it was the longest poem ever written by kids our age. Now we were going to send it off to Sir Alec Guinness, the movie star.

I felt a little uneasy about sending the poem to Mr. Guinness. For one thing, it said right on the cover of *The Guinness Book of World Records* that the author of the book was Norris McWhirter. But Wendy said that was probably just a pen name, and who but Mr. Guinness would write something called *The Guinness Book*?

So we borrowed *Talking to the Stars* from the library. It was a book full of addresses for movie and TV stars. Sure enough, Sir Alec Guinness was in there, on page thirty-eight. It said you could send letters to him in care of a television studio in England.

"Well," said Wendy, "this is it." It was another rainy afternoon, and Wendy, Carol, and I were up in Wendy's bedroom with the door closed. "All we need is a big envelope," continued Wendy. As she was talking, she began to edge her way off the canopy bed, tiptoeing toward her door.

"What are you—" Carol started to say, but Wendy gestured wildly for us to keep talking.

"Do—do you think Mr. Guinness will put the poem in his book?" I asked, never taking my eyes off Wendy.

"I don't know," said Carol, watching her, fascinated.

At this point, Wendy flung open the door, and

Katie fell into the room.

"Ow!" she shrieked indignantly.

"Caught you, you sneak!" cried Wendy.

"No fair," complained Katie, getting to her feet.

"No fair? *You're* the eavesdropper. I can't have any privacy in this house!"

"I just wanted to know what you were doing."

"Why didn't you knock on the door and ask us?"

"Because you wouldn't have let me in."

"Well, I'm certainly not going to let you in now. Go play with Scott."

Wendy slammed the door. "Boy, there's nothing but trouble in this house," she complained. "Scott's got a cold and he fusses all day. Katie is a darn sneak. My mother's been yelling at everyone lately, and Dad can't find another job. Even Miss Johnson's in a bad mood today."

"Your father hasn't had *any* luck with a new job?" asked Carol.

"Not a bit," replied Wendy.

I sighed. The three of us were getting less and less hopeful each day. The Whites weren't very hopeful, either. Mrs. White had started collecting cardboard boxes every time she went to the grocery store. And Miss Johnson had asked the kids to clean the junk out of their bedrooms so there'd be less to pack.

"Dad's got another job interview this afternoon," Wendy told us. She looked at her watch. "He's probably having it right now. There's a company in Ewing that needs someone. But Dad doesn't think he's the right person for the job."

Wendy started shuffling around the pages of the saga.

"Well, let's get back to Mr. Guinness," I suggested.

"Right," said Wendy. "Okay, the first thing we have to do is write a letter to him."

"Why?" I asked.

"So he knows why we're sending him the poem, stupid," snapped Wendy.

The room fell silent.

I stared at Wendy, stricken. Nobody had ever called me stupid. And Wendy had never called me *any* name, not even in teasing.

I told myself not to cry.

"Sara, I'm sorry," said Wendy. She looked helplessly at Carol. "I didn't mean to yell at you. I really didn't."

"It's okay," I said gruffly. I wished Wendy's father would hurry up and do something about his job. Not knowing what was going to happen was horrible. And it made Wendy impossible.

"Well, let's start the letter," said Carol brightly.

She pulled a sheet of flowered paper out of a drawer in Wendy's desk.

"Let's make it a real business letter," suggested Wendy, "the way Mrs. Fischer showed us at the beginning of the year. Do you remember how to do that, Sara?"

"Sure," I said. "Put the date and our return address in the upper corner. . . . No, the other one," I directed, watching Carol. Carol has the best penmanship of the three of us, so we let her write the letter.

"Now put down Mr. Guinness's address. . . . And now 'Dear Sir.'"

Half an hour later we were finished. This is what we said in our letter:

Dear Sir:

We are sending you a poem we have written. It is called "The Saga of Barbie and Ken." It is 350 stanzas long, and we think it is the longest poem ever written by kids. We really are kids, too. We are: Wendy White, 9 years and 10 months old; Sara Holland, 9 years and 8 months old; and Carol Holland, 10 years old.

Can you put our poem in your book? We think it breaks a record. This is the first record we've ever tried to break. If the poem is not long enough, just let us know. We can make it longer. We would really like to be in *The Guinness Book of World Records*.

Thank you very much for reading this. Please write to us soon. Wendy's address is at the top of the letter.

Yours truly,
Wendy White
Sara Holland
Carol Holland

"Now all we have to do is seal up the poem and mail if off," I said.

"Yeah!" smiled Wendy. "I can hardly believe it. We really did it!"

In the end, we had to put our poem in a big manila envelope. The saga was one hundred and twenty-one pages long, so it was very fat.

"We'll have to take it to the post office," I pointed out. "We can't put a regular old stamp on that. It'll probably need a whole lot of special stamps to go to England."

"Gosh, do you think it'll be expensive?" asked Carol.

"I don't know. Maybe. How much money do you have?"

"Just two dollars and thirty cents left over from my birthday."

"I've got one dollar and eighty-two cents," said Wendy. "I counted it this morning."

"Well, I've got three dollars and ninety-five cents," I said. "I've been saving my allowance. Let's see, how much do we have together?"

"Eight dollars and seven cents," replied Carol promptly. She's a math whiz.

"That should be enough, shouldn't it?" asked Wendy.

We nodded our heads.

"Let's mail it right now!" I cried, jumping up. "I can't wait."

"Whoa," said Wendy. "It's pouring. We'd have to ask one of our parents to drive us to the post office."

"Boo," I said, slumping back on the bed.

"We can do it tomorrow if it stops raining," suggested Carol.

"Okay," I said, brightening.

"Let's go get a snack," said Wendy.

We ran downstairs, passing Katie at the bottom.

"What are you doing?" she asked.

"Getting something to eat," said Wendy.

"Oh." Katie streaked up the stairs.

A few minutes later, armed with some nut bars,

we headed back to Wendy's room.

"Tiptoe," Wendy cautioned us.

Carol and I shrugged. "Okay."

We tiptoed up the stairs—just in time to see Katie sneaking out of Wendy's room.

"*What were you doing?*" thundered Wendy.

"Nothing," replied Katie guiltily.

"Katie, you are a DUMB OLD—"

"What's going on up there?" shouted Miss Johnson from the living room.

"Everything's FINE!" Katie screeched back.

"NO, IT ISN'T!" Wendy roared.

"WAHHH!" From somewhere nearby, Scott turned on the tears.

In the middle of all this, Mr. White came home.

He walked in the house to find Carol and me at the top of the stairs, our mouths stuffed with nut bars. Scott was crying, Miss Johnson was yelling at Wendy, Wendy was yelling at Katie, and Katie was yelling at everyone.

"What on earth . . . ?" he said, his face turning scarlet.

Immediately the yelling and crying stopped.

Carol and I swallowed our nut bars.

Wendy broke the silence. "Did you get the job?" she asked.

"NO!" Mr. White stomped up the stairs, ignoring

Carol and me. He slammed the bedroom door behind him.

"I didn't think so," said Wendy.

9.

Dress Rehearsal

Three days before the play, 4–B held its first dress rehearsal in the auditorium after school. It was a madhouse. A bunch of kids couldn't find the parts to their costumes. Two kids wanted to be in after-school sports instead of in the rehearsal. And Andy, in his Uncle Elmer costume with a beard and an old, frayed coat, was running around, chasing Sandy Murphy, who was Fido. Sandy was barking and growling and swishing the tail of his dog outfit.

In all honesty, Sandy didn't look much like a dog. He looked more like a big spotted mouse with mittens on. I pointed out to Mrs. Fischer that if she'd let me out of the play, I could do a much better job on Fido's costume. She just smiled, shook her head, and went back to pinning together Tom the Ragman's patched coat.

I looked down at my own costume. There wasn't much to it. Not that I was nude or anything. It was just that I was playing the part of a regular but sort of poor kid. So I was wearing everyday clothes that looked a little dirty and raggedy, plus a weird hat and clompy old shoes.

"GR-R-ROW-WOOF!" *Crash! Crash!* Uncle Elmer chased Fido near a chair and they both fell over it. Fido's tail came off.

I looked at Wendy, who was putting on Aunt Baldy's wig, and rolled my eyes.

"All *right*, people, that's enough!" shouted Mrs. Fischer, and everyone got quiet. A few of us even sat down. Mrs. Fischer hardly ever yells. When she does, you listen. We learned that way back last September. "Andrew," she said, "come sit down here next to me. Alexander, you stay where you are. Sara, please fix Alexander's tail. Stacey and Brett, cut the complaining. Everyone else, just keep your shirts on for a few minutes. We're almost ready to begin."

We settled down, and I got busy with a piece of wire and a needle and thread. Reattaching Fido's tail wasn't easy, especially with Fido inside the costume. There wasn't time for Sandy to take it off.

"Ow, you're pricking me!" he kept exclaiming, but I don't think I was.

I was tying the last knot when Mrs. Fischer called for our attention again.

"Will the people who appear in the first scene please go onstage?"

I broke the thread with my teeth and set Sandy free.

A chorus of complaints and questions rose up.

"I can't find my shoes, Mrs. Fischer."

"Mrs. Fischer, Brett stole my hat."

"I don't know where my place on the stage is."

"Am I in the first scene, Mrs. Fischer?"

It was another fifteen minutes before we were ready to rehearse Act I. I sagged into a chair and watched Wendy, Andy, Jackie Greenfield (who was playing Tom the Ragman), and Sandy wander around the stage.

Mrs. Fischer checked their costumes. When she was satisfied, she said, "If you feel ready, you may begin."

Wendy and Andy scooted offstage. We all looked at Jackie, who had the very first line in the play. He was supposed to say, "Ah, me, I am sooooo lonely," and let out a huge sigh. Instead he said, "Mrs. Fischer, I don't know where my play book is."

I groaned. If the whole rehearsal was going to go like this, we'd be here until tomorrow.

"Jackie, you're supposed to have your lines mem-

orized by now," Mrs. Fischer reminded him. "Please go ahead without your book. I'll prompt you if you forget anything."

"All right," said Jackie doubtfully. He paused. "Ah, me," he said finally. "I am so, so, so . . . so, sooooo . . ."

"*Lonely*," hissed Mrs. Fischer.

"Oh, right," said Jackie uncomfortably, his face turning pink. Everyone laughed. Even Mrs. Fischer was smiling.

I slumped further down into my seat, and my heart began to pound. Was everyone going to laugh at *me?* The dress rehearsal was getting closer to the real thing. It was the first time we had rehearsed with costumes and props and all the scenery. We had an audience, too. Practically the whole Art Club had stopped in to watch.

I couldn't concentrate on the play at all, even though Wendy was speaking now. I wished I were at home in my room with Star and Lucy. I would tell them fairy tales and they'd purr loudly. I'd kiss their noses and they'd nuzzle my face.

I closed my eyes and pressed my hands to my forehead. The sound of the play went on around me.

Suddenly I felt a light touch on my arm. "Sara?" asked a quiet voice. "You don't have to cry. It's going to be okay." I didn't recognize the voice.

I opened my eyes. Jennifer Sarason was sitting next to me.

I smiled at her. "I'm not crying. I was just thinking."

"About what?"

"Oh, lots of things. . . . Hey, your costume looks great."

Jennifer's character, the old woman named Rose, got her name because she always wore roses. So Jen's costume was a frumpy, saggy old dress with a corsage of plastic roses pinned to it. She had on a big straw hat covered with more plastic roses. I looked at her feet and saw she'd even stuck roses in her shoelaces. I giggled.

"What?" asked Jennifer.

I pointed to her feet.

Jennifer giggled, too.

I had to hand it to her. Of all the Deadbeats of 4–B, Jennifer was the most terrified of getting up on that stage. Even so, she was making sure her costume looked as good as possible.

Jennifer and I sat together during the rehearsing for Act I. Sometimes we talked, but mostly we just got nervous. By the time Mrs. Fischer called for the people in Act II, I was so scared my knees were wobbling. I stood up, and immediately had to sit down again. It was either that or fall down.

"Go on, Sara," Jennifer urged.

I stood shakily and teetered up the steps to the stage. I grabbed onto a rope for support. I hoped it wasn't attached to something up near the ceiling. Something that would come crashing down on me. Of course, if it did, I probably wouldn't have to be in the play. . . . Now, *there* was something to think about. Maybe I could arrange to break a leg sometime during the next three days.

I held my breath, waiting for a sandbag or a prop to zoom down and crush me. Nothing happened.

Unfortunately.

Mrs. Fischer called for Act II to begin.

Uncle Elmer started speaking.

I listened very carefully so I would know when to say my first line.

"Did you talk to Tom, Uncle Elmer?" I asked.

I was right on cue.

"Louder, Sara!" called Mrs. Fischer. "I couldn't hear you."

My cheeks burned. What did she want? I'd memorized my lines and come in on cue, hadn't I?

The play went on.

Truman pinched me.

"Cut it out, Truman," I said.

"Louder, Sara! And put some feeling into it."

I glanced out at the audience.

Jennifer smiled shyly at me. I felt better.

Finally the scene was almost over. I stood up from where I'd been sitting at the kitchen table so I could go to Elmer and say my last line.

Crunch! Thud! Yelp! Everyone began giggling except for Stacey Montgomery, who'd been sitting next to me at the table. Stacey started crying.

I looked around. My chair was on the floor. It had turned over when I stood up, and whacked Stacey on the funny bone.

"I can't move my elbow!" wailed Stacey.

"Klutz!" Andy yelled at me.

Mrs. Fischer rubbed her eyes wearily. "Okay, take a break," she said finally. "Stacey, come on. We'll see if we can find the nurse. Ten minutes, class, and then we'll do the last scene and go home."

I ran off the stage, my cheeks flaming. I ran right into Jennifer.

She grabbed my hand. "It's okay," she said. "It was just an accident. It won't happen again."

"It could," I sniffled. "I'm going home."

"But what about the last scene?"

"I can't do it. I just can't. I'm sorry, Jennifer. I'll see you tomorrow."

I shed as much of my costume as I could. I felt like setting fire to it. Then I ran most of the way home.

I went straight to my room and slammed my door.

Star and Lucy were asleep on my bed. The noise made them jump awake, but I barely noticed.

I threw my costume in my closet and stomped on it a couple of times. Then I lay down on my bed and burst into tears. Star padded over to me and nosed me worriedly. He purred in my ear. It tickled, but not enough to make me stop crying.

In fact, I began to cry so hard I didn't even hear my mother open the bedroom door.

"Sara?" she asked softly.

I turned my head and saw her standing uncertainly by my bed.

"What's wrong, sweetheart?"

I didn't want to tell her about the play, but I couldn't talk anyway, so it didn't matter. I cried harder.

"Daddy just got home. Do you want to talk to him?"

I did, but that was another problem. I hurt Mom's feelings when I talked things over with Daddy instead of with her. But what could I do about it? Mom and I always ended up arguing.

"Sara?"

I tried to stop gulping in air. "Can you tell Daddy to come in?" I said between hiccups.

"Of course," said Mom stiffly. Her eyes looked wounded.

She left the room. I felt like a little murderer, as if I had just taken aim and shot something at her. Something that killed a small part of her.

I closed my eyes. A few minutes later I heard Daddy come in. He sat on the edge of the bed and rubbed my back.

"Tell me why you're crying, punkin," he said.

"Rehearsal," I said through a fresh wave of tears.

"Rehearsal? You had a rehearsal today...and something happened?" asked Daddy.

"Yes." Somehow I got the whole story out.

"Pretty embarrassing," he said when I finished.

I nodded miserably.

"I guess there's nothing you can do, though," he went on. "I mean, that's what's nice about bad things. When they're over, they're over. No point in looking back on them. You can't change them. All you can do is move ahead—and maybe learn from your mistakes.... Did you learn anything today?"

"That I'm a klutz," I said. I sat up. The crying was stopping.

Daddy smiled at me. He touched my cheek with his finger. "Anything else?"

"Only that I'm a rotten actress. But I already knew that."

"That wasn't quite what I meant," Daddy said.

Lucy stepped daintily into my lap and turned

around twice before settling down. I stroked her fur.

Daddy changed the subject. "How's the saga coming?" he asked.

"Oh!" I cried. "I forgot to tell you. It's all finished!" I explained how we had written three hundred and fifty stanzas. Then I told him about mailing the saga to Sir Alec Guinness, which had cost most of our money.

When I finished, Daddy had a funny look on his face.

"What?" I asked him. "What is it?"

"Honey," said Daddy gently. "Explain again why you sent your poem to Sir Alec Guinness."

I told him about wanting to be in *The Guinness Book*, and how Wendy said Norris McWhirter was probably a pen name for Alec Guinness. I said we thought we could save ourselves a lot of trouble by sending the saga directly to Mr. Guinness.

"But Sara," said Daddy, "Sir Alec Guinness is a movie star. He has nothing to do with *The Guinness Book*. Norris McWhirter really *is* the author."

"Oh, no!" I cried.

"Don't worry, punkin. We'll just send another copy to the right place. I'm sure there's an address in *The Guinness Book*."

"Another copy?" I asked, feeling my skin grow crawly.

"Of course," said Daddy. "You do have another copy, don't you?"

I shook my head slowly.

"Uh-oh," said Daddy. "You should keep a copy of anything important you put in the mail. Even if you have the correct address, things can get lost. Once I mailed a birthday card to Uncle John. It took two and a half months to get across the street to him."

I groaned. "It's lost. It's *lost!* We can't remember all those stanzas."

"Now, don't get too upset about it. Yet," added Daddy. "Why don't you write to the TV station in London and ask them to watch out for your poem? Explain that you made a mistake. Send them enough stamps to mail the poem back to you."

"Okay," I said, leaping frantically off the bed, toppling Lucy to the floor in my rush. I had an awful lot to do. I had to call Wendy and Carol and tell them the news. Then we'd have to take *Talking to the Stars* out of the library again. And get together enough money for all that postage.

Oh, boy. We were in a real mess now.

10.

The Day before the Play

"Thank you, Elmer. Thank you," said Tom the Ragman.

"Aw, it was nothing." Uncle Elmer removed his hat and bowed his head modestly.

"Woof!" barked Sandy in his dog-mouse costume.

"Fido thanks you, too," explained Tom, patting Fido's head.

"It's a happy ending, a happy ending for everyone." Elmer sighed.

From downstage, Aunt Baldy growled something angrily.

"Well, almost everyone," Elmer corrected himself.

The townspeople began to clap and cheer, and the curtain came down on 4–B.

Our final dress rehearsal was just about over. Tomorrow would be the play, the real thing.

Mrs. Fischer hadn't said anything to me about running out of the rehearsal the other day. And I had gotten through the next two dress rehearsals okay. Well, I said my lines right on cue, anyway, but Mrs. Fischer told me I was still speaking too fast and too softly. I didn't care. The way I figured it, the faster I spoke, the faster I got through my part. As for talking too softly, I just couldn't bring myself to be any louder. I'd decided I would do nothing about it. Not even worry. I didn't care a fig whether the audience could hear me.

We took our bows the way Mrs. Fischer had shown us. Then I heard Mrs. Fischer clapping from her seat.

"Bravo!" she cried. "You did a fabulous job, class. If you do half this well tomorrow night, we'll be the hit of the festival. Now go home and get some rest. I'll see you tomorrow."

Jennifer and I looked at each other and let out our breath slowly. We grinned.

"After tomorrow it'll be all over," I said, "and we can really look forward to summer vacation."

Jennifer nodded. Then she said uncertainly, "Sara, I was wondering if . . . if maybe you could come over this weekend. I mean, if you want to. I mean . . . we could go swimming. We have this new pool. But if you don't want to—"

"I'd like to," I said before she could finish. "I'd like to go swimming." This was pretty neat. Nobody else I knew had a pool.

"Really?" asked Jennifer, sounding awfully surprised.

"Sure," I replied, but I felt sort of surprised myself. I, Sara Holland, had a brand-new friend.

"Wow! Great! See you tomorrow, Sara!" Jennifer ran off the stage.

"Hey, come on," I heard Wendy say behind me. "We better get going. We have an awful lot to do."

"Right," I said. Wendy and I got ourselves going.

On the way home we met up with Carol as planned. She was waiting for us by the No Parking sign on the corner of Beech Street and Marion Avenue. Her hands were empty.

"Where is it?" I cried.

"Hold on. I'll tell you everything," said Carol.

We were taking care of our *Guinness Book* problem. Yesterday after school we'd each done about a million chores trying to earn some money. Dad had given me a two-week advance on my allowance, and we'd written another letter to Sir Alec.

Today while Wendy and I were at rehearsal, Carol

had gone on two errands. "Okay," she said as we hurried home, "first I went to the post office. I have the stamps right here." She patted the back pocket of her shorts.

Carol had bought some more overseas stamps to send to Sir Alec. He could use them to return the saga to us.

"Then," she continued, "I went to the library, but I couldn't find *Talking to the Stars*. I asked the librarian where it was, and she said someone had taken it out. I asked her who, and she said she couldn't give out that information."

"Oh, no," Wendy and I moaned.

"I even told her it was an emergency, but I don't think she believed me. She said she could let us know when it was returned, and that was all."

"But that could be *weeks!* Anything could happen to the saga. Someone could throw it out. Sir Alec could lose it," I wailed.

We walked along in silence.

"What a day," said Wendy finally. "One bad thing after another."

"What else happened?" I asked.

"Oh," said Wendy, "it's Dad and his job. He has another interview this afternoon. An important one. And he's always in a rotten mood when he gets back from an interview. Also, this is his last chance. There aren't any more companies around here that he likes."

"You mean if he doesn't get this job, you'll have to move?" Carol asked, her voice rising.

I looked down at the ground, watching my feet move along. Left, right, left, right. I had a hole in one of my sneakers.

I didn't want to hear Wendy's answer.

"Yeah, probably," she said.

"Hey!" I said, brightening. "Maybe he'll get the job. Daddy always says, 'Think positive.' We should concentrate on your father getting this job."

"Maybe we should do a little white magic," suggested Carol. "You know, for good luck. Stop here a minute."

We stopped in the shade of a big tree and put our stuff on the ground.

"What's a lucky number?" asked Carol.

"Seven," I replied.

"Okay, everybody hold up seven fingers, and we'll chant, 'Mr. White will get the job,' seven times. Close your eyes to make it work."

So we closed our eyes and chanted. I thought we might have said it eight times, and I hoped it wouldn't make a difference.

"There," said Wendy when we finished. "I hope that helps."

"Me, too. What about *Talking to the Stars*, though?" I asked.

"Let's go to my room and think," Wendy replied.

We went to Wendy's room, taking some carob health cookies with us that Miss Johnson gave us in the kitchen. We didn't have to close the door. Katie and Scott were nowhere in sight.

"Now," said Wendy, "let's think about this. What could we do to get that address?"

"Find the book in another library?" I suggested.

"What other library?" asked Carol.

"Well, our school library probably wouldn't have it, but maybe the Ewing Public Library or the Clinton Public library would. Mom could take us in Hugh."

"I guess," said Wendy. She didn't sound too thrilled.

"Maybe we could find it in a bookstore," said Carol.

"Yeah, but somebody would have to drive us out to the mall," I reminded her.

"Oh. Yeah."

Wendy sighed. "I wanted to fix this up right away. I mean, this is so dumb. We've earned the money to mail the saga back, we've written to Sir Alec again. All we need is the address, and we don't have it because the stupid old librarian won't tell us where *Talking to the Stars* is. If we don't hurry up, we might never get our saga."

I thought Wendy was going to cry. She lay against her reading pillow, looking sad and sort of lost.

"Achoo!"

"Bless y—" Wendy started to say. "Hey, who sneezed?"

"Not me," I said.

"Not me," Carol said.

"Well, *I* didn't sneeze," said Wendy.

"Ah-ah-*choo!*"

"*Hey!*"

Wendy sprang off the bed and looked wildly around her room. Suddenly she flung up the pink coverlet and looked under her bed.

"I might have known!" she cried angrily. "Out! Get *out!*"

Katie squirmed sheepishly from under the bed. She looked a little dusty.

"I . . . swear . . . I . . . am . . . going . . . to . . . kill . . . you," Wendy said very slowly, as if Katie had a hearing problem.

"Wait—" said Katie desperately.

"Is Scott somewhere in here, too?" Wendy asked.

"I don't think so, but wait, I—"

"Where is he? Where *is* he?"

"He's probably next door at the Staneks', but—"

"Really?"

"Yes, yes. Wendy, listen. I can help you." Katie paused, expecting to be interrupted again, but nobody said anything. "See, you don't need to find *Talking to the Stars*."

"We don't?" Carol and I asked.

"No. I can give you the address."

"How do you know so much about all this?" demanded Wendy.

"From listening," Katie whispered.

"Oooh, you little—"

"Don't you want the address?" asked Katie sweetly.

"Of course we do. . . . How did you get it?"

Katie paused. I think she was trying to decide whether to look pleased with herself or guilty. "Remember when you caught me sneaking out of your room?" she asked.

"Yes," said Wendy. You could almost see the smoke coming out of her ears.

"Well, I wanted to know what you were doing, so I copied down the address on that big envelope while you were downstairs getting a snack. Your saga was in the envelope, wasn't it?"

"Yes," Wendy said finally, "it was." You'd have thought she'd have been a little happier. "I suppose you still have the address?"

"Sure," replied Katie. She ran into her room, then ran back and handed a wrinkled scrap of paper to Wendy. She looked very happy to have helped us out. "Aren't you going to thank me?" she asked. She looked from Wendy to Carol and me.

"*No*," said Wendy. "You're still a sneak. Go away and don't bother us."

Katie's chin quivered and her eyes filled with tears. She turned and walked out of the room, closing the door softly behind her.

"Don't you think that was kind of mean?" I asked Wendy.

Wendy glared at me. "Lay off, Sara," she said. "It's not your problem."

"What do you mean, it's not my problem?" I said. Suddenly I felt good and angry at Wendy. Maybe she was my best friend, and maybe she was upset about moving, but I was sick and tired of her being rude whenever she felt like it.

"It is too my problem, Wendy White," I said loudly. "We're all in this together. I am trying very hard to get the saga back, and all you do is mope and complain. I'm going home now. I'll mail the letter this afternoon. Goodbye."

I stood up.

Wendy was gazing at me, horrified. When she

found her voice, she said, "Sara . . . Sara, wait. I'm sorry. You're right. . . ." She still looked as if I'd just sprouted a second nose. "I've never heard you talk like that before."

Neither had I, for that matter. "Well," I said. "Well . . . maybe it's about time I began sticking up for myself. After all, you're not going to be around to do it for me."

Silence.

I glanced at Carol. She began sniffling and dabbing at her eyes.

Wendy started to cry, too. "I wanted the three of us in *The Guinness Book* so *badly*," she wailed. "It would have been like a—a tribute to our friendship. We would all be in there together. And then, after I've moved away, it would be like saying Carol and Wendy and Sara were best friends. It would be in print and it would be forever."

"Oh, Wendy," I said. Now I was dabbing at my own eyes. "Maybe it'll still get in. I think it might. This letter should get the saga back, and then we'll start over again. . . . You know what you said about a tribute to our friendship? That was nice."

Wendy gulped and blew her nose.

Carol and I blew our noses, too.

We sat around and sniffled for a while.

After a few minutes, Wendy got up and opened

her door. She peeked out. Katie's door was shut. Wendy knocked on it and disappeared inside. When she came out, Katie was with her and they both looked much happier.

"Let's go wait for Dad to come home," suggested Wendy.

The four of us ran downstairs and stationed ourselves on the front porch. When Mr. White finally drove up the driveway, we stampeded to his car. We pounced on him as soon as he opened the door.

"Did you get the job, Daddy?" cried Katie.

"Did you get it?" asked Wendy.

I crossed as many of my fingers and toes as I could, and scrunched up my eyes, hoping. Please say yes, please say yes, I said over and over to myself.

I opened my eyes.

Mr. White looked very tired. He mopped his brow with a dingy handkerchief. "Don't know, lambs," he replied. "I won't know until tomorrow. But I wouldn't set your hearts on it."

"Oh." Wendy's face fell.

"Daddy," Katie ventured, "can you play catch with me?"

"Not now, baby. I'm very tired. You kids play outside and let me rest until Mommy comes home, okay?"

"Okay."

Wendy offered to play catch with Katie. But Katie said she didn't feel like playing anymore, so we sat on the steps.

Just sat.

We sat there until my mother called me in for dinner.

"Goodbye," I said sadly as I stood up to leave. And then, "Goodbye, Wendy," I whispered as I ran home.

11.

"Uncle Elmer's Fabulous Idea"

The next morning I woke up slowly. I lay in my warm bed, rubbing my eyes and remembering a dream. Wendy and I had been walking down Beech Street. Our pockets were full of dimes and quarters. We were on our way to Jugtown, the best candy store in all of Riverside. Suddenly, without actually walking there, we were standing in front of the candy case inside Jugtown, our noses pressed to the glass. We were looking at the goodies spread out in front of us. Mr. Curtis, the store owner, was behind the counter, his back to us. We gazed at the bins of jawbreakers, licorice sticks, Mary Janes, root beer barrels, and gumdrops. I couldn't make up my mind. Finally I turned to Wendy and said, "You go first."

Wendy opened her mouth to start talking, and

Mr. Curtis turned around. Only he wasn't Mr. Curtis. He was Wendy's father.

"Time to go now, lamb," he said. "It's moving day."

And the next thing I knew, Wendy and Mr. White had disappeared and I was alone in Jugtown.

I rolled over and buried my head under the pillow.

Then I remembered the play. It didn't make me any happier.

And then I remembered what had happened when I got home from Wendy's house yesterday.

Triple whammy.

I'd run in the door and sat down breathlessly at the table.

"Wash your hands," Mom had reminded me.

I sighed loudly.

"Don't take that attitude with me, young lady," Mom snapped.

She had gotten up on the wrong side of the bed that morning and had been crabby all day.

I washed my hands at the kitchen sink and sat down again.

Mom eyed me critically but couldn't find anything else wrong.

"Well," said Daddy. "Well."

Silence.

"You know what I'm going to do this summer?"

I announced, trying to fill the empty spaces.

"What?" asked Daddy.

"I'm going to learn how to knit. Then I'll knit sweaters for Staz and Lulu."

"I hope you're going to do more than that," said my mother. "I hope you plan to get outdoors a bit."

"Liz," warned Daddy.

"Chris," warned my mother.

I started to warn both of them but thought better of it. I put my fork down. It was getting hard to eat.

"Are you ready for the play tomorrow?" my mother finally asked. She sounded slightly friendlier.

"I guess," I said.

"You certainly don't sound very excited about it."

"Well . . ."

"You won't give in, will you?" exclaimed Mom suddenly. "You're determined to be unhappy."

"What? I don't un—"

"For pity's sake, Liz, enough is enough!" Daddy banged his fist on the table. I half expected him to send Mom to her room.

"And why do you always take *her* side?" cried Mom. "I want her to be happy. I want her to have friends. I want her to join in. That's all."

"I do have friends," I said quietly. "I have Wendy

and Carol and Star and Lucy."

"Oh, swell," said Mom bitterly. "Your cousin, a girl who's about to move away, and two cats. That's terrific, Sara, just terrific."

"Excuse me," I said, and left the table without waiting to be excused officially.

I retreated to my room. I knew Mom wouldn't be speaking to me for a while.

I flumped down on my bed and thought. These days, the whole entire world was grouchy. I wondered if I could stand up to my mother the way I'd stood up to Wendy. It probably wouldn't be a great idea. But maybe I could try something different. Usually, when Mom was ignoring me, I kept quiet, too, waiting for her to get over being angry. But if I made the first move and talked to her, she'd look pretty silly not answering her own child.

Before I went to bed I worked out a plan for talking to Mom. Then I rehearsed it in my head, as if it were a play. Maybe Uncle Elmer had taught me something after all.

So here I was, the next morning, lying around in bed, not wanting to get up. I sighed, rolled over, threw on some clothes, and went down to breakfast.

"Morning, honey," said Dad.

"Morning," I replied.

Mom was eating scrambled eggs. She didn't look

up from her plate.

I decided to put the plan I'd thought of into action. "Well, today's the day of the play. Are you still coming, Mom?" I bet she couldn't ignore a direct question.

"Oh, yes. Of course," she answered quickly.

"Good. I thought maybe since you weren't talking to me, you might not come."

Mom looked at me, surprised. Daddy, too, and I thought I saw a warning in his eyes.

I rushed on. "I'm glad you're coming, because I really want you there. It'll make me feel better. . . . Gosh, I better go or I'll be late."

I scrambled around for my lunch box and book bag. As I ran across the lawn to Wendy, I looked over my shoulder at the front door. Mom and Daddy were watching me. Mom waved. I waved back.

Wendy and I ran all the way home from school that afternoon. We didn't have a rehearsal, and we were dying to find out whether Mr. White had gotten the job. He wasn't home, of course, but we thought he might have called Miss Johnson, or—or we weren't sure what. We were just hoping good news would be waiting for us at the Whites'.

But there was no news.

"You could call him at work," I suggested.

Wendy shook her head. "Nope. He said he can't talk about this at the office."

"Oh. Well, we'll just have to wait. It's three-fifteen. We have to be back at school at six to get ready for the festival. What time will your dad get home?"

"Around five-thirty."

"Good!" I cried. "We'll know before the play."

Wendy and I spent the afternoon fidgeting. We were nervous about the play, anxious to hear Mr. White's news, and worried about our saga. I think we drove Miss Johnson crazy.

We made Jell-O and spilled the whole bowl on the floor. We bounced Ping-Pong balls off the walls in the den until we gave Miss Johnson a headache. We watched cartoons standing on our heads until we gave ourselves headaches.

Five-fifteen came, and no Mr. White.

Five-thirty came, and no Mr. White.

"Wendy, I have to go home," I said at last. "Mom's making me eat dinner before the festival. I'll meet you out front at ten of six and we'll walk to school together."

Wendy nodded miserably.

I dashed home and changed out of my school clothes.

Mom was in the kitchen when I went downstairs. She had set a tuna-fish sandwich at my place at the table. "All ready?" she asked.

I nodded and took a teensy bite out of the sandwich. I wasn't hungry at all.

"Nervous?" she asked.

I didn't answer. I pretended I hadn't heard. "Be there by a quarter to seven so you can get good seats," I said. "Are you sure Daddy will get home in time?"

"Positive," said Mom. She kissed my forehead. "That's for good luck."

I guess she was over being crabby.

By ten of six I'd eaten only a quarter of the sandwich, but Mom let me leave anyway. "Do your best!" she called after me as I went to meet Wendy.

Wendy and I arrived at school at 6:05. Mr. White hadn't come home, and Wendy was a wreck. Also, she'd suddenly gotten really scared about her part in the play. I think it was because yesterday the Riverside Elementary baseball team had stopped in to watch our final rehearsal and Wendy had forgotten her lines a couple of times. She was afraid it would happen tonight. Mrs. Fischer had said, "Bad rehearsal, good performance," or something like that, but Wendy didn't feel any better.

Our play was going to be the last feature in the June Festival. We had to wait until almost 7:45 before we went onstage. That gave me plenty of time to panic.

The girls put on their costumes in 4–B, and the boys put theirs on in 4–A. That took about ten minutes. Then we all gathered in 4–B. Mrs. Fischer checked our costumes. A few kids grabbed play books and looked at their lines one last time. Wendy went off in a corner to study her lines alone.

And I did a very stupid thing. I told Mrs. Fischer I needed a drink of water. Then I crept down the hall and peeped through the door to the auditorium.

It was full. Packed, to be exact. It was stuffed with mothers and fathers and brothers and sisters and grandmas and grandpas and aunts and uncles and neighbors. Adults were standing in the back, and kids were sitting in the aisles and windowsills. Where had they all come from? There were at least six hundred and forty eyes. Maybe more.

I let the door silently swing closed. Then I ran into the girls' room and stood around waiting to throw up. But nothing happened. I was glad I hadn't eaten much dinner.

Finally I went back to 4–B. I had to talk to Mrs. Fischer.

Three kids were already waiting to talk to her. One of them was Jennifer. She was crying.

I pulled her aside. "What's wrong, Jen?"

"I can't do this." She sniffled. "I'm not going on that stage in front of all those people."

I handed Jennifer a tissue from the box on Mrs. Fischer's desk. What was I supposed to say? I'd been about to tell Mrs. Fischer the very same thing. But Jennifer needed somebody to stick by her.

"Look, Jen, we'll go out there together," I told her. "You can hold my hand during the last scene if you want. I don't think anyone will notice. We'll say our lines, and then it will be all over. I'll go swimming at your house, and we'll have the whole long summer to goof around in." That'll show my mother, I thought. I had a real friend who wasn't moving away, and who wasn't a cousin or a cat.

"Okay," said Jennifer, but she didn't sound too happy. She stopped crying, though.

At 7:40, Mrs. Fischer lined us up and walked us down the hall to the door that led backstage. The curtain fell on 3 – A and their recorder recital, and the third-graders scampered offstage. Jackie and Sandy took their places, while Mrs. Fischer went around in front of the curtain to announce "Uncle Elmer's Fabulous Idea" to the audience.

Then the curtain rose, Jackie said, "Ah, me, I am sooooo lonely," and the play was under way.

During the first act, Jennifer and I huddled together, gripping hands and listening. Wendy didn't forget any of her lines.

The curtain came down on Act I and the audience applauded loudly. I turned to Jen and grinned. They liked our play!

But now it was time for *me* to go out on the stage.

"Good luck!" whispered Jen earnestly. "I'll see you in Act Three."

I nodded. My knees did their Jell-O thing and my stomach did flip-flops. I took my seat at Baldy and Elmer's kitchen table. All I could think of was dumping my chair over and whonking Stacey Montgomery's funny bone.

In a few seconds, the nieces and nephews and Baldy and Elmer were ready.

This was it.

The curtain rose and I waited to see the six hundred and forty eyes.

Instead I saw only blackness.

I blinked.

The lights onstage were so bright, and the rest of the auditorium was so dark, I could barely see past the first two rows.

Act II began.

I listened very carefully, determined not to miss my first line.

Please, God, I prayed, don't let me do anything stupid.

"Well, I went to town today," said Elmer.

That was my cue.

"Did you talk to Tom, Uncle Elmer?" I asked.

I could almost hear Mrs. Fischer saying, "Louder, Sara."

The play continued.

I felt a pinch on my arm.

"Cutitout Truman," I said. Definitely too fast and too soft. And absolutely without feeling. Oh, well.

"Elmer, you idiot!" called Aunt Baldy from the stove.

That was the beginning of a long speech of Baldy's, right before my next line. My eyes were used to the light now, so I searched the audience. Down in the fourth row, I spotted my parents and Wendy's family. Daddy was watching the play thoughtfully, but Mom was watching me. And she was smiling. I smiled back.

But I was puzzled. Didn't she care that I'd said my line too fast? I didn't think I'd done my best. Or maybe I had.

I heard my next cue.

Very, very, very carefully I eased my chair back. I stood up as if I were eighty-seven years old.

I didn't hear any crashes or yelps.

I walked to Uncle Elmer, put my hand on his shoulder—and froze.

What was I supposed to say? I'd been concentrating so hard on not being a klutz that I couldn't think of my line.

Luckily, Andy saved me.

"*I* think . . ." he prompted me in a whisper.

My face was on fire. "Ithinkit'sawonderfulidea-Uncle."

The audience rustled. They probably hadn't heard me.

Too bad for them.

The curtain came down and I breathed easier.

Two more lines to go and it would be over.

The last act began. Jennifer and I stood together and held hands, as I'd promised her. When the curtain rose this time, I wasn't startled by the bright lights. But Jen was. She gripped my hand.

"Tom's an old fool if he won't listen to my uncle," I said on cue.

"He'll listen," replied Jen, a little too loudly.

The townspeople jeered and cheered.

The audience laughed.

"ListentohimTom." My last line!

"Keep trying, Elmer," said Jennifer. She was supposed to sound excited, but instead she sounded dull. And nervous.

Who cared, though? The play was *over* as far as Jen and I were concerned. Over, over, over! I couldn't resist squeezing her hand and grinning. I almost giggled. The only thing left was the curtain call. Then we'd be free forever. Or at least until September. The play would end, and Mom and Daddy and I would go out to celebrate. Then Mr. White would tell us he'd gotten the job. And if he didn't, I'd have Jen, and she and I would have fun together all summer long, and maybe she'd get to know Carol, too. Oh, and of course the saga would turn up, and eventually it would be published in *The Guinness Book*.

"It's a happy ending, a happy ending for everyone," Elmer said with a sigh, and his hat fell down over his eyes.

The audience chuckled.

Aunt Baldy growled and muttered angrily. I could tell Wendy was just dying to wave her arms around.

"Well, almost everyone."

I clapped my hands along with the rest of the townspeople.

Then the audience began to clap. They clapped while the curtain came down. They clapped while Wendy, Andy, Jackie, Sandy, and the nieces and nephews took their bows. And they clapped while the townspeople took their bows. A few moments later, when 4–B was gathered backstage, they were still clapping. Mrs. Fischer came over to me and put her arm around my shoulders. "I knew you could

do it," she said.

I grinned.

Then I spotted Jennifer. "Jen," I said, "I'll talk to you tomorrow about swimming, okay?"

She nodded eagerly.

"I have to find my parents. 'Bye!" I called.

"'Bye, Sara!"

I found Wendy and helped her get her wig off. Then we pushed our way through the people in the corridor. It was so crowded we couldn't find our parents, so we decided to change out of our costumes first. We finally found everyone outside the auditorium.

"You were wonderful, punkin," Daddy said, hugging me.

I was?

"The play was great," added Mom.

"Thanks," I said. "You really liked it?"

"Really."

"I said my lines too fast—and I almost *forgot* one."

"Well," said Mom, "they were a little fast. But you got up on that stage and pitched in and were part of things."

Just like she wanted.

"I'm not sure I did my best." I don't know why I had to say that. I was challenging Mom, just when we were getting along okay.

"Did you purposely say your lines too fast?" she asked.

"No!" I cried.

"Then I think you were doing your best. Listen, we can talk about this more later. Right now, how about a chocolate soda? We thought we'd go to Ichabod's."

"All of us?" I asked. "The Whites, too?"

"All of us," said Dad.

"Yay!"

We walked over to Ichabod's in a big group. Katie and Scott ran and screeched and leaped around the whole way. They were pretty excited about having ice cream, what with eating Miss Johnson's health food most of the time.

"Dad!" said Wendy suddenly, "did you get the job?"

"No," said Mr. White slowly.

Wendy's face fell. Mine probably did, too. Now the Whites would move. Soon. Well, I thought, I had Jen now. And Carol. And Wendy and I could write letters. And maybe our saga would get published. I remembered my dream, with Mr. White saying, "Time to go now, lamb. It's moving day."

Then I realized Mr. White was talking for real. "But," he was saying, "when I told my boss this morning that I was thinking of leaving the company because I don't want to move, he said he didn't want to lose me. I can keep my job here. No transfer! How about that?"

"No transfer!" shouted Wendy. "No transfer! All *right!*"

"Oh, boy!" I shouted. I jumped up and down and hugged Wendy. I couldn't believe it. The play was over, I had a new friend *and* I had Wendy! What a summer this was going to be!

At home that night, Mom and Daddy and I sat around in the living room. Star and Lucy joined us. Star climbed in my lap. I petted him slowly and he closed his eyes and purred his rumbly purr.

I closed my eyes, too. I was proud of myself for having gotten through the play. I'd never be an actress, that was for sure. But the next time I had to get up in front of people, I probably wouldn't hate it so much.

"Well," said Mom, "it's all over."

I nodded.

"Was it as bad as you thought it would be?"

I opened my eyes in time to see Daddy flash that warning look at Mom.

"Mom," I said, "if I answer you honestly, are you going to get mad?"

Mom looked hurt. "No," she said.

"All right. I didn't enjoy the play. It wasn't fun at all. It ruined the last few weeks for me. I'm glad it's over and I hope I never have to be in another play. . . . But it wasn't as bad as I thought it would be."

"Oh," said Mom. "Well . . . you really didn't enjoy it?"

"I *really* didn't. Mom, how come you make me do so many things I don't want to do?"

"We've been through that. It's because I want you to be happy."

"What if Daddy said you had to start taking horseback riding lessons so you could be happy?"

"That's ridiculous, Sara. I can't stand horses. That wouldn't make me happy."

"Well, I feel the same way about plays . . . and parties."

Mom paused. "All right, you've made your point."

"You're mad, aren't you?"

Daddy and I looked at her carefully.

"No," said Mom finally. "But Sara, I want you to know that I don't push you just to be mean. As you get older you're not going to be able to avoid parties and groups of people. And tonight you learned what you can do when you have to."

I nodded. "You're right."

Mom and I smiled at each other tiredly. "Good night, everybody," I said. I stood up, gathering Star in my arms, and headed for bed with Lucy at my heels.

After the Play

One hot day, a couple of weeks after the play, Wendy let herself into our house and found me reading a book in the den with Lucy sound asleep in my lap. Wendy was smiling from ear to ear and holding an envelope.

"Guess what!" she cried, moving over so she could stand in front of the air conditioner.

"What?"

"Something came in the mail today," she sang, waving the envelope under my nose.

"What?"

"Something wonderful."

"What?"

"Something you won't believe."

"WHAT?"

Wendy smiled smugly. "Our saga's back," she said at last.

"Really? This is our saga?" I tried to grab it from her, but she held it tight.

"Something else came with the saga."

"What? What? What?"

"A letter from Sir Alec."

"Oh, let me see!" I couldn't stand the suspense any longer.

Neither could Wendy. Suddenly she tore open the envelope and handed me a sheet of white paper. "He wrote to us *personally*, Sara. You and Carol and me. He says he liked our poem very much. He says it has *potential*. And he says he's sorry he doesn't have anything to do with *The Guinness Book*, but that he believes we'll be poetesses one day. Imagine that. Us. Poetesses."

"You know what I think?" I said.

"What?" asked Wendy.

"I think that since we have the saga back, we should add those fifty stanzas to it. I mean, don't you think real poetesses would?"

"Yeah," said Wendy. "That's a good idea. But you know what I think we should do first? I think we should make a copy of the saga."

"*Two* copies," I said.

"Let's get Carol," shouted Wendy, already running to the front door.

"And Jen."

"Okay," said Wendy.

I said goodbye to Star and Lucy, and went off to join my friends.

About the Author

Ann M. Martin grew up in Princeton, New Jersey, and was graduated from Smith College. She lives in New York City, where she works as a free-lance writer. Other books by Ms. Martin include *Bummer Summer* and *Inside Out*, also available as Apple Paperbacks.

Look for these and other **Apple Paperbacks**
in your local bookstore!

BUMMER SUMMER

Ann M. Martin

There's nothing worse than feeling left out. . . .

Summer is supposed to be the best time of the year. But
this summer looks like a total loss to Kammy Whitlock.
First, her dad gets married again. Then, his new wife Kate
moves in, and Kammy has to put up with her two children.
They won't leave Kammy alone! Three-year-old Muffin
flushes Kammy's best paints down the toilet, almost stran-
gles her cat, and the baby cries for hours at a time.

Camp has always sounded hateful. But when Dad and
Kate suggest that Kammy go away to Camp Arrowhead,
Kammy figures it can't be worse than staying home. How
wrong can a person be? Arrowhead is a disaster. Now the
only question is: What can Kammy do to save the summer
from being a total bummer?

ISBN 0-590-33139-6/$1.95US/$2.25CAN

INSIDE OUT
Ann M. Martin

It wasn't easy having a brother like James. . . .

It's not much fun when you take your four-year-old brother to the playground and he starts eating gravel. Or when you can't get to sleep at night because he spends it screaming. Or when the kids at school tease you about having a brother who's a retardo.

But that's what it's like for Jonno.

His little brother James is autistic. And lately it seems that everything's getting spoiled because of James. Jonno just wants to be normal — he's tired of being laughed at by the "in-kids." And if that means forgetting about James or other people's feelings, who cares? Shouldn't Jonno get a chance to think about himself for a while?

ISBN 0-590-33552-9/$2.25US/$2.95CAN

JUST PLAIN CAT
Nancy K. Robinson

Someone let a Tiger loose in the house!

Chris never thought that a seven-week-old ball of fur could make such a difference in his life. But Tiger, his new kitten, manages to change everything! First of all, his stuck-up neighbor, Veronica, is no longer the only cat-owner around! Then, nothing is safe from Tiger — from his father's darkroom to his mother's newly varnished floor!

Everything else seems to be changing, too. Chris's best friend, Peter, is moved to a different reading group, his new third grade teacher is the dreaded Mrs. Marmelstein, and his father gets a big job — to photograph a life-size dollhouse.

Will things ever be normal again?

ISBN 0-590-31782-2/$1.95US/$2.25CAN

THE HOT
AND COLD SUMMER
Johanna Hurwitz

Crazy things start to happen when Bolivia comes to town!

Rory and Derek are best friends forever. . . . At least that's what they think — until they meet Bolivia. She's visiting next door all summer and everyone wants the three of them to be buddies. But since she's a *girl*, Rory and Derek decide to ignore her completely. Except it's not so easy to ignore someone who has her own pet parrot and who likes to make snowballs — out of ice-cream!

Derek starts thinking Bolivia's the funniest, craziest kid he's ever met, but Rory still says three's a crowd. Is there room in their friendship for Bolivia, or is she about to break up a perfect team?

ISBN 0-590-33572-3/$2.25US/$2.95CAN